Gifted & Talented®

Still More
Questions & Answers

For Ages 4–6

By Kathie Sweeney, M.A.

Illustrated by Larry Nolte

LOWELL HOUSE JUVENILE

LOS ANGELES

CONTEMPORARY BOOKS

CHICAGO

*Heartfelt thanks to my husband, Rich, my beloved children,
Stephanie and Craig, and to the very special soulmates who
together circle me with love and inspiration.*

—K.S.

Reviewed and endorsed by Joanne López, M.A., veteran elementary educator and
member of the National Association for Gifted Children

ISBN: 1-56565-748-9

President and Publisher: Jack Artenstein
Director of Publishing Services: Rena Copperman
Executive Managing Editor, Juvenile: Brenda Pope-Ostrow
Editor in Chief, Juvenile: Amy Downing
Director of Art Production: Bret Perry
Editor: Jessica Oifer

Lowell House books can be purchased at special discounts
when ordered in bulk for premiums and special sales.
Contact Department TC at the following address:
Lowell House Juvenile
2020 Avenue of the Stars, Suite 300
Los Angeles, CA 90067

Manufactured in the United States of America

10 9 8 7 6 5 4 3 2 1

Note to Parents

Teach a child facts and you give her knowledge. Teach her to think and you give her wisdom. This is the principle behind the entire series of *Gifted & Talented®* materials. And this is the reason that thinking skills are being stressed in classrooms throughout the country.

The questions and answers in the **Gifted & Talented® Question & Answer** books have been designed specifically to promote the development of critical and creative thinking skills. Each page features one "topic question" that is answered above a corresponding picture. This topic provides the springboard to the following questions on the page.

Each of these six related questions focuses on a different higher-level thinking skill. The skills include knowledge and recall, comprehension, deduction, inference, sequencing, prediction, classification, analyzing, problem solving, and creative expansion.

The topic question, answer, and artwork contain the answers or clues to the answers for some of the other questions. Certain questions, however, can only be answered by relating the topic to other facts that your child may already know. At the back of the book are suggested answers to help you guide your child.

Effective questioning has been used to develop a child's intellectual gifts since the time of Socrates. Certainly, it is the most common teaching technique in classrooms today. But asking questions isn't as easy as it looks! Here are a few tips to keep in mind that will help you and your child use this book more effectively:

★ First of all, let your child flip through the book and select the questions and pictures that interest him or her. If the child wants to do only one page, that's fine. If he or she wants to answer only some of the questions on a page, save the others for another time.

★ Unlike most books, this book does not have to be read sequentially. Each page is totally self-contained. Start at the back, the front, the middle—the choice is up to your child!

★ Give your child time to think! Wait at least 10 seconds before you offer any help. You'd be surprised how little time many parents and teachers give a child to think before jumping right in and answering a question themselves.

★ Help your child by restating or rephrasing the question if necessary. But again, make sure you pause and give the child time to answer first. Also, don't ask the same question over and over! Go on to another question, or use hints to prompt your child when needed.

★ Encourage your child to give more details or expand upon answers by asking questions such as "What made you say that?" or "Why do you think so?"

★ This book will not only teach your child about many things, but it will teach *you* a lot about your child. Make the most of your time together—and have fun!

The answers at the back of the book are to be used as a guide. Sometimes your child may come up with an answer that is different but still a good answer. Remember, the principle behind all *Gifted & Talented*® materials is to **teach your child to think**—not just to give answers.

How did the teddy bear get its name?

The teddy bear is named after President Theodore (Teddy) Roosevelt, the 26th president of the United States. In 1902, President Roosevelt went bear hunting, and the hunting dogs cornered a bear cub. The cub was so frightened, President Roosevelt felt sorry for it. Though his companions shot the bear, a newspaper cartoon showed the president's compassion. A New York store owner made a stuffed bear, placed it in his store window with the cartoon, and named it "Teddy's Bear." This huggable stuffed bear became an instant success.

1. Why do you think people like teddy bears so much?
2. How can you find out more about teddy bears?
3. What are some names of different types of real bears? Where can you go to learn about them?
4. Why do you think calling the stuffed bear "Teddy's Bear" helped sell so many of the toys?
5. What are your favorite stuffed animals? Why?
6. What other name can you think of for a teddy bear? Why is that a good name?

Why do we have drums in our ears?

Each of our ears has an eardrum inside it to help us hear different sounds. The eardrum is a very thin material, called a *membrane,* that stretches across the middle ear and separates it from the outer ear. When sound hits the eardrum, it vibrates. This vibration, or movement, makes three tiny bones inside the ear wobble. Together, these parts of the ear allow us to hear.

1. If you have two ears, how many eardrums do you have?
2. When you have an earache, who should you see to have it checked?
3. Why is it important to listen carefully in school?
4. How is an eardrum like the musical instrument we call a drum?
5. Where might you see people playing drums?
6. If you were going to be in a parade, what instrument would you like to play?

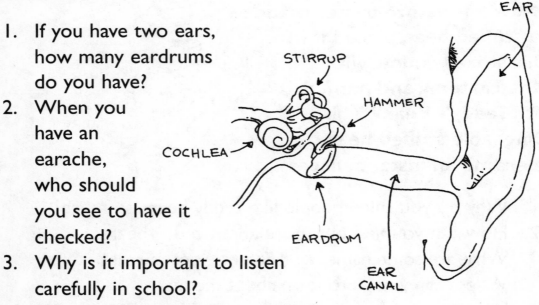

What is the tallest building in the United States?

The tallest building in the United States is the Sears Tower in Chicago, Illinois. It has 110 stories and is 1,454 feet high. There are 18 escalators and 16,000 windows in the building. It took four years to complete the structure. On a clear day, you can see four different states from its top—Indiana, Michigan, Wisconsin, and Iowa. On windy days, people inside the tower can actually feel the building sway slightly.

1. What do you think it would feel like to be in an office on the 110th floor on a windy day?
2. Where are other tall buildings like the Sears Tower located? If you do not know, how can you find out?
3. What is the tallest building that you can build with your blocks or Legos? Compare its height to your knees, waist, shoulders, or head.
4. Why is it important for a tall building to have a sturdy and solid base?
5. In what ways are tall buildings and short buildings alike?
6. On a separate piece of paper, can you design a funhouse for children?

Where were puppets first created?

It is believed that the first puppets came from either Egypt or India. The oldest known puppet theaters have been found in these countries. Today, there are many different types of puppets: hand puppets, finger puppets, shadow puppets, rod puppets, and marionettes.

1. Have you ever seen a puppet show? When? Where?
2. Which type of puppet is your favorite? Why?
3. Why can a girl or a boy provide the voice for any puppet, no matter if the puppet is male or female?
4. Why is *Pinocchio*, shown in the picture, a great story to perform using a marionette?
5. Why do you think shy people might feel more comfortable performing in a puppet show than being onstage themselves?
6. How can you use a brown paper bag to create your own puppet? Remember to use markers, paints, and any other materials to decorate your puppet.

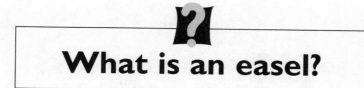

What is an easel?

An easel is a three-legged stand used by artists to hold their canvases as they paint. It was invented by a Dutch artist in the 17th century. The Dutch people called this invention an *ezel* because they thought it looked like a donkey. The Dutch word for donkey is *ezel*. The English borrowed this word and changed the spelling to *easel*.

1. Why do you think it is easier to paint at an easel than on a flat tabletop?
2. What kinds of pictures do you like to paint?
3. What colors do you like to use the most when you paint?
4. Because the donkey is related to the horse, it is often called a "cousin" of the horse. Do you have any cousins? How many? What are their names?

5. Where do Dutch people live? Can you find this place on a globe or a map? Ask an adult if you need help.
6. On a separate piece of paper, can you design a blue ribbon for the first-place winner in an art contest?

Why are some people ticklish?

There are tiny nerve endings hidden under the surface of the skin. When these nerve endings pick up even the lightest touch, they send a message to the brain. The brain then decides how this feels. Some people's brains may think certain touches are ticklish, while other people's brains may think those touches are itchy or painful. This is why only some people are ticklish.

1. Are you ticklish? Where are you most ticklish?
2. Have you ever been tickled too much? When? Why did it seem like too much?
3. If a person's mind can make him or her feel more ticklish, how can someone try to stop being so ticklish?
4. Can you tickle yourself? Try it, and ask family members to try it, too. Is it possible?
5. How many ways can you think of to tickle someone? Make a list on a separate piece of paper.
6. On a separate piece of paper, can you design your very own tickle machine?

Why do we sneeze?

We sneeze to get rid of dust and germs that are trapped inside the nose in a space called the *nasal cavity*. The walls of this space are covered with a sticky liquid called *mucus*. This mucus helps trap the dust and germs that are in the air so they don't enter our bodies. We sneeze to get rid of them. Sometimes certain plants, animals, and smells bother a person's nose and make that person sneeze.

1. Do you sneeze loudly or softly? Do you sneeze only once or many times in a row?
2. What types of things make people sneeze?
3. Why do people cover their mouths when they sneeze?
4. What are allergies? Why do you think a person with allergies might sneeze more than other people at certain times?
5. Your nasal cavity is a passageway to your lungs. What might happen to your lungs if you didn't sneeze out dust and germs?
6. Can you make up a funny story about someone who can't stop sneezing? Why does he or she keep sneezing? Tell your story to a friend or a family member.

Why do we yawn?

People yawn when they are tired, bored, or need some more oxygen. A yawn is a deep breath that brings more oxygen into our bodies. This oxygen makes us feel more awake. Yawning also helps us wake up because when we yawn, our face and neck muscles stretch. This stretching makes more blood and oxygen move, or *circulate,* around our bodies. If a person yawns over and over again, it means he or she is very tired.

1. What other animals, besides people, yawn?
2. Why do you think people cover their mouths when they yawn?
3. If you yawn around other people, what do you think might happen? Try it and see.
4. How else can you bring more oxygen into your body besides yawning?
5. Why is it dangerous to stay awake for too long?
6. What can you find out about the character Rip Van Winkle, who slept for many years?

Why do some people have freckles?

Freckles are caused by a special coloring in the skin called *melanin*. People with a lot of melanin have dark skin. People with less melanin have lighter skin. People with freckles have more melanin in some parts of their skin than in other parts. Exposure to sunlight causes our bodies to make more melanin. That is why people can get more freckles after being exposed to the Sun for a while.

... 84, 85, 86, 87, 88...

1. Do you know any people who have freckles? Who?
2. What color skin and hair do these people have?
3. Do you think people can stop their skin from developing freckles? Why or why not?
4. What can you tell about the amount of melanin in a person's skin if his or her skin is dark? What if a person's skin is very light?
5. What else can the Sun do to a person's skin?
6. How can you protect your skin from the Sun?

Are every person's fingerprints the same?

No, each person is born with his or her own unique set of fingerprints. Even identical twins have different sets of fingerprints. Our prints never change throughout our lifetime. Scientists don't know why we have different prints. In the late 1800s, Sir Francis Galton, an English scientist, proved that no two fingerprints are alike. The pattern of loops, arches, or whorls (spiral-shaped marks) seen on fingerprints is different on every person.

1. On what objects around your house have you accidentally left fingerprint marks?
2. What is the easiest way to clean fingerprints off a window?
3. What can you do to help keep your fingerprints off windows, television screens, and mirrors?
4. Why do the police use fingerprints to identify people?

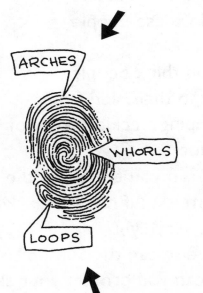

5. Have you ever had your fingerprints taken? When? Where?

6. Do other animals, besides humans, have fingerprints?

One Step Further

Use washable ink pads to make little characters out of your fingerprints. Press your finger onto the ink pad and then onto a separate piece of paper. Using colored pencils or markers, add a head, a face, ears, arms, legs, feet, and whatever else you need to create animals or little people with your prints. What will you name each one?

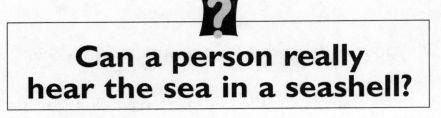

Can a person really hear the sea in a seashell?

When you hold a seashell up to your ear, you might hear a sound similar to waves crashing on the beach. But you are not actually hearing the ocean. Blood is always flowing around inside your head. The seashell's hard, smooth surface bounces, or *echoes*, the sound of the flowing blood back into your ears. This sound is very much like the sound of the ocean.

1. Have you ever listened to the sound in a seashell? What did it sound like to you? Did it sound loud or soft?

2. Where can you find seashells?

3. What animals have shells covering their bodies?

4. What types of food do people eat that have shells?

5. Why do you think people like to collect shells?

6. Can you think of some words that begin with the **sh** sound? Make a list on a separate piece of paper.

How did the Ferris wheel get its name?

The Ferris wheel was named after an American inventor named George Washington Gale Ferris. He designed the first Ferris wheel, which was 250 feet high and could hold 2,160 passengers at one time. It was first ridden at the World's Columbian Exposition in Chicago, Illinois, on June 21, 1893.

Today the Ferris wheel looks very much like Ferris's original design and remains quite popular.

1. In what state is the city of Chicago? Find this state on a globe or a map.
2. Have you ever ridden a Ferris wheel? How did it feel?
3. What do you think a two-story Ferris wheel might look like?
4. The largest Ferris wheel today can hold 480 people at one time. How many more people could the first Ferris wheel hold? If you need help, ask an adult.
5. Can you make a list of objects with wheels that you can ride?
6. What are your favorite rides at an amusement park, a carnival, or a fair?

What is a queen?

A queen is a woman who is a leader of her country. She can lead either with her husband, a king, or by herself. Kings and queens become leaders because they are born into a royal family. Once a woman is the queen of her country, she usually will stay queen for the rest of her life. Great Britain, the Netherlands, and Spain are three countries that have royal families.

1. What job do you think a queen might have?

2. How can you learn more about queens and kings throughout history?

3. What would you do if you were the queen or king of a country for a day?

4. What do you think the word **royal** means? What are a prince and a princess? If you do not know, how can you find out?

5. Does the United States have a royal family? If not, who rules the country?

6. The bees in a beehive work for the queen bee. How is the queen bee like the queen of a country?

One Step Further

Have an adult help you create a royal castle out of a cereal box. Gather a cereal box, colored paper, paper towel tubes, scissors, tape, glue, and crayons. Then use your imagination and go to work. How will you use all the objects you have collected to make a great castle? Include a castle door, stones on the castle walls, and a lot of windows. You might even want to create a moat around your castle. When you are done with the castle, make a queen and a king to live in it!

Why does a snail leave a shiny trail as it moves?

A snail leaves a shiny trail behind it because it releases a sticky fluid, called *mucus,* from the bottom of its body as it moves. A snail uses a large muscle under its shell, called a *foot,* to move. This foot must be moist, or wet, in order for a snail to be able to move. The mucus keeps the foot moist. This mucus is so sticky it helps snails crawl on even very smooth surfaces, such as glass. As this fluid dries, it leaves a shiny, slimy mark.

1. Have you ever picked up a snail? What did it feel like?
2. Where are you most likely to find snails?
3. What other legless creatures travel by contracting their muscles?

4. How can a snail climb up a thin, smooth blade of grass?
5. How can you measure a snail's journey in your yard or in front of your home?
6. Pretend you run a snail circus. Can you think of four amazing feats a snail could perform with its sticky fluid? What are they?

How do ants talk to each other?

Ants talk to each other, or *communicate*, by rubbing their *feelers* together. Feelers are the long, thin antennae on the top of an ant's head. Ants live in underground nests called *colonies*. Each ant in a colony has a specific job to perform, so it is very important that they communicate.

1. Where have you seen ants?
2. Have ants ever invaded your home? Where in your home did you find them?
3. What does it feel like to have an ant crawling on your skin?
4. What do you think ants are "saying" to one another when they rub their feelers together?
5. Why do you think an ant might sometimes bite you?
6. **Aunt** is a word that sounds like the insect **ant** but has a different meaning. Do you have a favorite aunt?

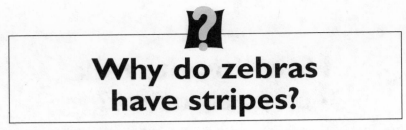

Why do zebras have stripes?

A zebra has stripes so that it can *camouflage,* or hide, itself in the grasslands where it lives. When a zebra's enemy, called a *predator,* is nearby, a zebra can easily hide by blending in with the tall, wavy grasses. Also, when a group of zebras run from a predator together, all of their stripes blend together and look blurry. This makes it difficult for the enemy to single out just one zebra to attack.

1. Have you seen a live zebra? Where?
2. What other animals have stripes? How many can you name?
3. Why do you think zebras in the United States live in zoos?
4. If you wanted to hide yourself in the jungle, what would you wear?

5. A zebra's stripes are like our fingerprints—no two zebras are exactly the same. How could you use this fact to help you keep track of a group of zebras in a wild animal park?
6. Think about what the word **camouflage** means. Why do you think a leopard has spots or an alligator's body is shaped like a log?

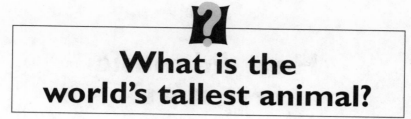

What is the world's tallest animal?

The giraffe is the tallest animal in the world. The tallest recorded height of a giraffe was 20 feet. The average giraffe is about 14 feet to 18 feet tall. The giraffe's long neck allows it to eat leaves from the high branches of a tree. The giraffe also is able to spot danger from great distances because it can see over the tall trees in the grasslands.

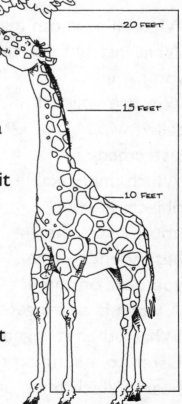

1. What do you find most interesting about a giraffe?
2. How is an ostrich like a giraffe?
3. How do you think the spots on a giraffe help protect it from its enemies in the grasslands where it lives?
4. What helpful jobs around your house or school do you think a giraffe could perform?
5. If a giraffe spots danger from far away and then begins to run, what might this tell other animals near it?
6. What type of house would you build for a giraffe? What would you use to build it?

How did music first start?

No one knows for sure when music first began. We do know that singing began as soon as people began to speak. Hunting tools were used as some of the first instruments. In France, carved bones that appear to be wind or percussion instruments date back to about 25,000 B.C. The first written music dates back to at least 800 B.C.!

1. What animals can make music?
2. What instruments can you name?
3. Why are whistles called wind instruments?
4. Which unbreakable objects in your house make the best sounds when you beat on them?

5. A violin is a stringed instrument. What other stringed instruments can you name?
6. Listen to a song on the radio. Which instruments can you hear? Which ones are your favorites? Why?

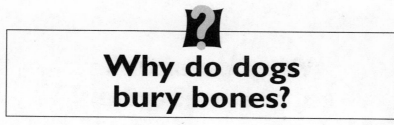

Why do dogs bury bones?

Dogs bury bones to hide them from other animals. They also hide bones to save for food later. This is done by *instinct,* which means that they were born to act this way. Their *ancestors,* or the wild dogs that lived before them, also buried bones. Dogs are able to remember the exact spot where they bury their bones by a scent they leave. This way, they can return to the same place and find their bones.

1. Why do you think people have dogs as pets?
2. What are some special jobs or tricks that people can train dogs to do?
3. How many different kinds of dogs can you name?
4. What do you do with food you want to save for later?
5. Where would you bury a bone if you were a dog? Explain your answer.

6. Can you explain the expression "a dog is man's best friend"? Draw a picture on a separate piece of paper to illustrate your explanation.

Why do skunks sometimes smell?

A skunk doesn't always smell, but when it is defending itself, it often releases a terrible-smelling spray. When a skunk feels scared or threatened by another animal, it stamps its feet, arches its back, and hisses. If the animal doesn't leave, the skunk raises its tail and squirts out a smelly liquid called *spray*. **If the spray gets in the other animal's eyes, it blinds the animal for a few minutes.**

1. Skunks are nocturnal. What does this mean?
2. An octopus also squirts out a liquid to protect itself. How does this liquid spray work like a skunk's spray?
3. An animal's fur or skin coloring often helps hide or protect it. How does a skunk's black-and-white coloring help protect it at night?

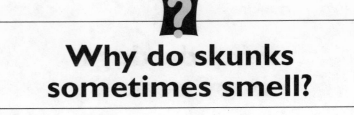

4. What do you think the expression "that smells like a skunk" means?
5. A skunk that is seen in daylight is probably sick and might try to bite a nearby person. What would be the best thing for you to do if you saw a skunk in the daytime?
6. A skunklike smell is added to odorless gas in order to warn people if a gas tank is leaking. What other ways can you think of for using a skunklike smell?

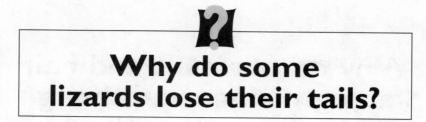

Why do some lizards lose their tails?

A lizard can lose its tail as a way of protecting itself. If an enemy sneaks up on a lizard, the lizard might quickly run to safety. But if an enemy grabs the lizard by the tail, the tail comes off. It is either left in the mouth of the enemy or wiggles about on the ground, distracting the enemy. Meanwhile, the lizard escapes. It can grow its tail back at least once in its lifetime, and it can also live without its tail.

1. A lizard is a reptile. What other reptiles can you name?
2. Lizards are cold-blooded and need the Sun to keep warm. What do you think the weather is usually like where lizards live?
3. Keeping in mind that lizards are cold-blooded, what would you need to be careful about if you wanted to keep one as a pet?

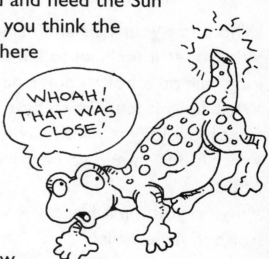

4. What do lizards eat? How can you find out?
5. How are lizards able to camouflage, or hide, themselves?
6. Can you tell a story about a lizard who escaped from danger without losing its tail?

Why do our nails and hair keep growing even though we keep cutting them?

Cutting our hair and nails only trims away the dead ends. The parts of our hair and nails that are alive are underneath the skin. It is from here that they continue to grow. Hair and nails are made of protein. We need to eat foods containing protein in order to keep our nails and hair strong. Good sources of protein include fish, meat, eggs, and milk.

1. Who trims your hair and nails?
2. What does it feel like to have long hair on a hot summer day? What does it feel like to have short hair? How long is your hair?
3. What foods should you eat to keep your hair and nails healthy?
4. Why do you think Halloween witches often have long hair and fingernails?
5. How does long hair help protect a person from cold weather?
6. On a separate piece of paper, can you draw a person who hasn't cut his or her hair or nails in many, many years?

Where did the word *bangs* come from?

Hairstylists took the style and name of bangs from champion horses whose tails had been "banged off." In the early 1900s, stable boys found they could save time while grooming a horse by cutting the horse's tail in a short, square style. This way, they didn't have to do as much brushing. They called this "banging off" the tail. Years later, hairstylists used this grooming technique to create a new hairstyle.

1. Do you have bangs? Who do you know who has bangs?
2. Why do some parents think cutting bangs on a child can save time?
3. If it doesn't hurt to have your hair cut, do you think it hurts the horse to have its tail banged off?
4. What other jobs does a stable person do when taking care of a horse?

5. If you had a horse, what would you name it? How would you style its mane and tail?
6. How do you think the ponytail hairstyle began?

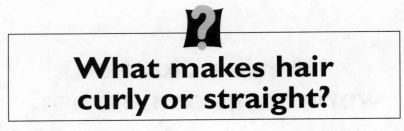

What makes hair curly or straight?

Hair grows from a root under our skin. The root grows inside a tiny hole, or pit, called a *follicle*. The shape of the follicle is what makes hair curly, wavy, or straight. If the follicle is oval, then hair grows curly. If the follicle is kidney-shaped, then hair grows wavy. Hair grows straight when the follicle is round.

1. What type of hair do you have?
2. What kind of hair follicles must be under your skin to grow your type of hair?
3. What special color and type of hair would you choose if you could change your hair for one week? Why?
4. Can people with curly hair make their hair straight? How?
5. What animals have curly or wavy hair?
6. Why do people have different hair colors? How can you learn more about this?

One Step Further

Can you make a graph of all the different hair types in your family? Ask an adult to help you make a chart like the one below. Then color in one square for each person with straight hair, one square for each person with curly hair, and one square for each person with wavy hair. If you have a small family, add some of your friends' names to the chart. Use a different color crayon, marker, or pencil to color each type.

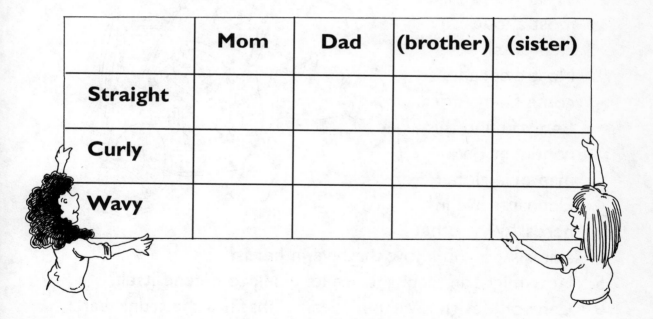

	Mom	**Dad**	**(brother)**	**(sister)**
Straight				
Curly				
Wavy				

Is an elephant's trunk like the trunk of a car?

No, but it is just as useful! An elephant really doesn't pack anything in its trunk, but it can use its trunk like a hand to pick up and hold on to things. It can pick up a tiny peanut and hold a baby elephant's tail with its trunk. It also uses its trunk to drink water, to strip bark and leaves from trees, and as a hose to wash itself.

1. What types of things would you pack in an elephant's lunch?
2. What do you like most about elephants?
3. Most elephants come from Africa. Can you find this continent on a map or a globe?
4. Elephants live in herds. What other animals do you know that live in herds?
5. How might an elephant use its trunk to defend itself?
6. Can you design a vacuum cleaner that has the trunk, ears, tusk, and tail of an elephant? Draw your idea on a separate piece of paper.

? Where does mold come from?

Mold comes from *spores*. Spores are in the air all the time. In order for mold to grow, the spores must land in an area that is damp and fairly dark, and can provide food. Mold lives off food made or left by plants, animals, and rotting materials. Mold is neither a plant nor an animal. It is part of a special group of living things called *fungi*.

1. Where have you seen mold growing? Why do you think it was growing there?
2. What colors come to mind when you think of mold? Why?
3. Does mold need sunlight to grow?
4. In what places in your house do you think mold would grow best?
5. Why do you think mold might grow on damp clothes in your closet or on wet sneakers under your bed?
6. If you wanted to do a science project on mold for school, how could you make mold grow on food?

Why does my body sometimes get shocked?

People sometimes feel a shock when an electric charge jumps from one place to another. *Static electricity* is an electric charge that does not move. Instead, it builds up in one place. Your body carries electric charges, too. A charge can build up when you walk across a carpet or pull a sweater over your head. When you touch an object or even another person, the charge jumps to that object or person.

1. How do we use electricity every day?
2. When have you felt static electricity?
3. What happens if you touch someone right after you drag your feet across a carpet?
4. On a separate piece of paper, can you draw a picture of yourself making sparks of static electricity fly?

5. What do you think people used for heat and light before electricity was discovered?
6. What things would you miss most if you didn't have electricity?

What makes water boil?

When water gets very hot, it boils. Water is made of *molecules*. Molecules are groups of *atoms* joined together. Heat causes these molecules to move faster and faster. As the molecules speed up, they move farther apart. When this happens, water boils. Water is a liquid. When it freezes, it changes to a solid called *ice*.

1. Why do people boil water?
2. Why should you be very careful when you are near a pot of boiling water on a stove?
3. Do you think water molecules speed up or slow down as water freezes? Why? Explain your answer.
4. What would happen if you heated ice cubes?
5. What happens to the molecules in ice cream as it is made? What is your favorite flavor of ice cream?
6. Can you draw an ice-cream sundae large enough to feed an entire classroom of children? Draw it on a separate piece of paper.

Where was ice cream first made?

Ice cream was first made in Asia many, many years ago. In 1295, Marco Polo, an Italian explorer, brought the recipe for this delicious treat back to Italy from Asia. Ice cream soon became popular all over the world. In 1851, Jacob Fussell opened the first ice-cream factory, where this treat was made in large amounts. In the 1900s, refrigerator-freezers were invented, making it easier to store and keep ice cream in homes.

1. Can you find Italy on a map or a globe? On what continent is it located?
2. When do people usually eat ice cream?
3. What is your favorite way to eat ice cream? What are your favorite flavors?
4. Why was it easier to keep ice cream in homes after refrigerator-freezers were invented?
5. Why do you think Americans celebrate birthdays with cake and ice cream?
6. Can you make up a story about how or why the custom of giving birthday presents began?

? Why does a sponge soak up water?

A sponge soaks up water because it has many tiny *airholes,* or spaces. These airholes act as straws and *absorb,* or suck up, the water. When we squeeze the water out of a sponge, we empty the airholes.

1. How are sponges used in your home?
2. Look at the mops used in your home and school. What materials are they made of? How do these materials make it easier to clean floors?
3. Why do you think people throw sponges away after they have been used for awhile and replace them with new ones?
4. Where are sponges found in nature? If you don't know, how could you find out?
5. Why can one sponge absorb more water than one paper towel?
6. How much heavier is a wet sponge than a dry sponge? Weigh them to find out.

Why do I feel dizzy when I spin?

When you spin around in a circle, the liquid deep inside your ears swishes around. This movement tells your brain that your body is spinning, and so you feel dizzy. When you stop spinning, the liquid continues to swish around, and the brain still thinks you are moving. This is why you still feel dizzy even after you stop spinning.

1. What things on the playground make you feel dizzy when you ride them?
2. What else besides spinning makes you feel dizzy?
3. If someone says to you, "I think you're dizzy," what do you think he or she means?

4. What type of people spin around when they perform for an audience?
5. What objects or toys spin?
6. Spin around in a circle, then hold your hands together in front of your eyes and stare at them. What happens? Wait five minutes, then spin again. This time, do not look at your hands when you stop. What is different?

How did the french fry get its name?

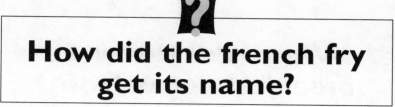

The french fry got its name because it originally came from France. The french fry was brought to the United States in the early 1800s by Thomas Jefferson, the third president. While in France, Jefferson sampled these sliced potatoes and became quite fond of them. He asked for the recipe so that he could serve them to his friends when he returned to America.

1. What do you usually eat with your french fries?
2. What other ways are potatoes served?
3. How does a carrot grow like a potato?
4. What are a potato's eyes? Can a potato see with its eyes?
5. If you were a farmer and wanted to plant more potatoes, you would use each eye of the potato to start a new plant. Look at a potato. How many plants can you start with it?
6. How do you think so many foods, words, customs, and holiday celebrations came from other countries to America?

Where did the word *breakfast* come from?

The word *breakfast* was first used in 1463. The word *fast* means to go for a long period of time without eating. We fast from the time we go to bed until we wake up in the morning and eat. This time period is much longer than the break between breakfast and lunch or between lunch and dinner. We stop, or *break*, this fast with our first meal of the day. This is why we call the morning meal breakfast.

1. Which foods do people usually eat in the morning?
2. Which breakfast food is your favorite? Why?
3. If you were going on an early morning hike and had to pack breakfast to take with you, what would you pack?
4. What can you feed a toothless baby for breakfast?
5. Why do you think breakfast is the most important meal of the day?
6. If you were going to serve your parents breakfast in bed, what would you serve them?

❓ Is there really a man in the Moon?

No, there is not really a man in the Moon, but sometimes it looks like there is one. Large mountains and deep craters are on the surface of the Moon. These mountains and craters sometimes create shadows on the Moon's surface. From the Earth, these shadows look like a face, which we call the "man in the Moon."

1. Do you think people can live on the Moon? Why or why not?
2. The Moon has different shapes at different times of the month. What shapes have you seen?
3. Which shape of the Moon is your favorite? How can you find out what your favorite shape is called?
4. What two things would you like to learn about the Moon?
5. Why is it easier to see in the dark on a clear night when the Moon is full?
6. If you were an astronaut who discovered little Moon creatures, what "earthly" gifts would you give them so they could learn more about life on Earth?

What is a solar eclipse?

A solar eclipse is when the Moon blocks all or part of the Sun's light from a specific area on the Earth. This happens because the Moon comes between the Earth and the Sun. During a total eclipse, all of the Sun's light is blocked by the Moon, and the Earth becomes dark for a few moments. When the outer edges of the Sun are still showing, it is only a partial eclipse. Though the Sun doesn't seem as bright during an eclipse, its rays are just as strong. They can damage our eyes, so don't ever look up at an eclipse.

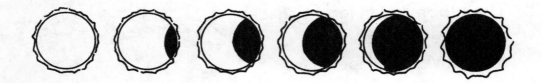

1. Which stage of the solar eclipse above shows a total eclipse? How do you know?
2. Why do you think people are so curious about space, the Sun, the Moon, and the stars?

3. Why might animals become quiet and still in the darkness of a total solar eclipse?

4. Look at a large object that is far away, then close one eye. Hold your thumb in front of the other eye. The object should be hidden by your thumb. How is this similar to a solar eclipse?

5. If the Moon is smaller than the Sun, why do you think it can block out the Sun from the Earth?

6. Why do you think people wear sunglasses?

One Step Further

Ask an adult to help you make your own model of an eclipse. Place a tennis or similar size ball into an empty glass. This ball will be the Earth. For the Moon, roll a piece of clay into a ball about the size of a Ping-Pong ball and stick a pencil into it. Use a flashlight for the Sun. Hold the Moon (clay ball) in between the Sun (flashlight) and the Earth (tennis ball) to make an eclipse. Your adult friend may need to hold one of the objects.

What is solar power?

Solar power is energy from the heat of the **Sun** that has been collected and saved. Two special sets of containers or tanks are used to capture and store this energy. A liquid is pumped through the first set of containers. When the Sun beams down on them, it makes the liquid hot. The liquid is then piped to the second set of tanks, which contain sand or gravel. These tanks hold the heat so it can be used at a later time as energy. People use solar power to create electricity, cook food, and heat or cool their homes.

1. What are some items in your house that need energy to work?
2. Why do you think some people use solar power instead of electricity made by an electric company?
3. People also gather energy from other natural sources. Have you ever seen a windmill, a waterwheel, or a hot-air balloon? Where? What kind of energy do these instruments trap?
4. What are other ways that people use the Sun?
5. If you buy a plant that needs a lot of sunlight to grow, where in your house would you keep it?
6. On what kind of day is it easiest to catch solar energy? Explain your answer.

When were flags first invented?

The oldest flags were made about 3000 B.C. in ancient India, China, and Egypt. A flag is a symbol that stands for something, such as a country or an organization. Each state in the United States has its own flag. Families in the Middle Ages (500–1500 A.D.) used flags, shields, or family crests to stand for, or *represent,* them. Today, many groups have their own symbol or flag to represent them.

1. Where do you usually see flags?
2. What colors and designs are on the American flag?
3. Which state flag is your favorite? Where could you look to find out what all the state flags look like?
4. In the library, what symbols can you find that represent the Boy Scouts, the Girl Scouts, or the Olympic Games?
5. Why do you think certain groups like to have their own special flag?

6. What colors and designs would you put on your own personal flag? Draw one on a separate piece of paper.

Where did the word *telephone* come from?

Alexander Graham Bell invented the telephone when he was 29 years old in the year 1876. He also made up the word *telephone*. In the Greek language, *tele* means "a far distance." *Phone* means "sound." Bell's invention was able to carry sounds for long distances, so he put these two Greek words together to form the word *telephone*.

1. What other words can you think of that have **tele** in them?
2. People use a telephone to communicate. What are other ways that we communicate?
3. What is your telephone number? Why is it important to know your own telephone number?

4. How many different types of phones can you name?

5. Have you ever played the game "Telephone"? Why does the message often change as it gets passed around?

6. Who do you call if there is a fire or if someone is in danger?

One Step Further

Alexander Graham Bell invented the telephone after he heard sounds come through the wires of a telegraph. Can you make your own telephone using a piece of string and two plastic cups? Poke a hole inside each cup that is just large enough to fit the string. Put each end of the string through each hole and tie a knot inside the cups to secure the string. Have someone hold one of the cups to his or her ear while you talk into the other cup. Be sure to hold the string as tight as possible. Take turns talking and listening. How do you think your voice travels from one cup to the other? How is this like a real phone?

❓ Why do people blush?

When people feel embarrassed, surprised, angry, afraid, or excited, they often blush. These feelings tell the brain to send extra blood to the face. Tiny blood vessels in the skin grow larger as they fill with blood. This brings more blood to the surface of the skin. When the blood shows through the skin, it looks reddish. This is what we call *blushing*.

1. Have you ever blushed? Why?
2. When have you seen someone blush? What do you think made that person blush?
3. What types of things or situations make you blush in front of other people?
4. How do you think actors and actresses make themselves look like they are blushing?
5. Have you ever used makeup on your face? When?
6. On a separate piece of paper, can you draw a picture of a red-cheeked clown?

Where is my funny bone?

Your funny bone really isn't a bone at all. It is a nerve found just under the skin of your elbow. A *nerve* is like a wire that sends messages between the body and the brain. When you hit the bone at the back of your elbow on a table or other object, the nerve between your skin and bone sends a message to the brain. This message shouts, "Ouch, that hurts!"

1. What part of your body is like your elbow?
2. Have you ever banged your funny bone? What did it feel like?
3. Can you point to all these parts on your body?
   - ankle
   - wrist
   - neck
   - knee
   - elbow
   - chest
   - hip
   - shoulder
   - waist
4. Can you think of a better and more accurate name for the funny bone?
5. What types of food have bones attached to them?
6. If your friend just banged his or her funny bone, what would you do to make that friend feel better?

YOW!
GASP
PANT!
Hee Hee!!

What are baby teeth?

Baby teeth are the first set of teeth a person has. When we are about six months old, these baby teeth begin to push up through our gums. By around age three, we have a complete set of baby teeth. Permanent teeth start to replace baby teeth when we are about six years old. If we take care of our permanent teeth, we can keep them for the rest of our lives.

1. How old were you when your parents discovered your first baby tooth?

2. Do you have any permanent teeth yet? How many do you have? Where are they in your mouth?

3. What does it mean when a baby is teething? Do other baby animals teethe?

4. How can you take good care of your teeth?

5. Have you heard of the tooth fairy? What does the tooth fairy do? What do you think the tooth fairy looks like?

6. Can you draw funny faces with unusual teeth on a separate piece of paper? Witches, goblins, vampires, and jack-o'-lanterns are all fun characters to draw.

How do whales sleep?

Whales do not sleep through the night like we do. Scientists believe that whales take several short naps each day. These naps are only about two or three hours long. Whales sleep just below the surface of the water. Their blowhole is the only part of their body that stays above the water's surface. This way, they can use their blowhole to breathe as they sleep.

1. Where can you go to see whales? Have you ever seen a sleeping whale?
2. A whale breathes using the air above the water. How does a shark breathe underneath the water?
3. Why is it dangerous for people to fall asleep in water?
4. In what position do you sleep? Do you have a special sleep toy? What is it?
5. How do you swim differently from a fish?
6. If you were going to make a sea mattress for a whale to use as a bed, what materials would you use? Draw a picture of it on a separate piece of paper.

Why does a whale spout water?

A whale spouts water when it blows air out through its blowhole. The blowhole is a small opening at the top of the whale's head that acts like a nose to help the whale breathe in and out. Though whales live underwater, they need air to breathe, like humans do. Whales can stay under the water for up to two hours without coming up for a breath of air.

1. What do whales eat?
2. How many different types of whales are there? How can you find out?
3. What do you find most interesting about whales?
4. A fish can breathe through its gills underwater. How is a whale different from a fish?
5. Where can you go to see and learn about whales?
6. What would happen to a whale if it became trapped underwater? Can you tell someone a story about how you freed a trapped whale?

Do cowboys really exist?

Yes, cowboys still exist today and so do cowgirls! They are workers, *or hired hands,* who tend cattle. During the middle to late 1800s, cowboys and cowgirls helped settle the American Wild West. Cowboys and cowgirls are known for wearing large hats, boots, and *chaps,* which are leather flaps worn over jeans.

1. How can you find out about cowboys and cowgirls who helped settle the Wild West? Who are some famous people who lived in the Wild West?
2. What types of jobs do you think cowboys or cowgirls might do during a day's work?

3. What are cattle?
4. What is a cow magnet? How can you find out?
5. What types of food come from cows? What food comes from cattle?
6. Each ranch marks its cows and cattle with a different symbol or design to show who owns them. This is called **branding**. Can you create a brand or a design for a ranch of your own? Draw it on a separate piece of paper.

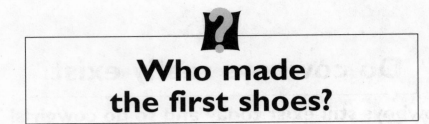

Who made the first shoes?

No one is exactly sure who made the first shoes. But we know that ancient Egyptians wore sandals as early as 3700 B.C. These early sandals were made of grass, animal skins, or wood. Baglike foot wrappings made of animal fur were the first closed shoes worn by people living in colder areas.

1. Can you name different types of shoes? What are they?
2. Why do you think different materials are used in making shoes and slippers?
3. Why do you think horses wear horseshoes?
4. What is your favorite kind of shoe to wear?
5. What do you put on your feet when you go to the beach?
6. What do cats and dogs have on the bottoms of their feet that help to protect their feet?

? Why do onions make people cry?

Slicing or chopping an onion makes people's eyes water. The strong smell comes from an oil that seeps out as an onion is peeled and cut. This oil turns into a vapor, or mist, that rises into the air and affects the eyes. If the onion is held under running water while being peeled, the amount of vapor is reduced. The water breaks up the vapor and washes some of it down the drain. This can prevent tears when the onion is being chopped.

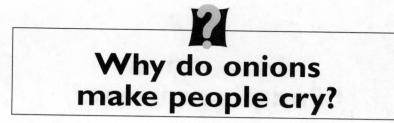

1. Do you like onions in your food? Do you prefer raw onions or cooked onions?
2. What foods do you usually eat with onions?
3. Why is an onion called a **root vegetable**?
4. What other foods have their skin peeled away before being eaten?
5. Why else do people cry?
6. What things help you to feel better when you are crying?

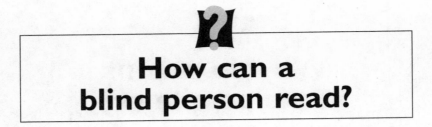

How can a blind person read?

A blind person can read by using something called *braille*. In 1824, Louis Braille, a 15-year-old blind French boy, invented the braille system. (It was not published until 1829.) He placed raised dots on wooden blocks so that blind people could read by feeling with their fingertips. These dots form different patterns to make the braille alphabet. Blind people can read and write using this system.

1. What do blind people use to help them get around?
2. If you couldn't see, how could you help yourself learn about things in the world around you?
3. Why do you think some people wear glasses?
4. Why do you think people should have their eyes checked regularly? How does a doctor examine children's eyes?
5. What are some games that you play while blindfolded?
6. Can you write your name in braille?
   You might want to go to the library and find a book on the braille alphabet to help you.

What is noise pollution?

Noise pollution is simply too much noise. When the space around you becomes too loud, it can be annoying or even harmful to your ears. A busy city might have constant noise created by cars, trucks, buses, trains, and heavy machinery. A busy office building might be filled with machines, phones, radios, and people's voices. Noise pollution can cause people to feel tired, have headaches, or be unable to concentrate on their work.

1. How do you feel when it's too noisy around you?
2. Where is there a lot of noise pollution? Why do you think it is so noisy in these places?
3. Where can you go inside your home to find peace and quiet?
4. What can you do to make sure your house is not full of noise pollution?
5. What are other types of pollution you have learned about?

6. If you had a magic vacuum cleaner that could suck away anything that causes too much noise, what two items would you suck up?

Do soap bubbles have a color?

A soap bubble often looks clear, but it is actually filled with all the colors of the rainbow. When light shines on a bubble, you can see all these colors. The colors swirl and bounce around inside the bubble. We call this quality *iridescence*.

1. When have you played with bubbles? What was the most fun about it?
2. Where have you seen bubbles? Make a list of these places.
3. When you watch a bubble float through the air, what happens to it eventually? Why do you think this happens?
4. Will you see more color in a bubble on a dark, rainy day or on a bright, sunny day? Why?
5. Why do you think bubbles make people laugh and play?
6. What ingredients do you need to make bubbles?

Answers

PAGE 5

1. Sample answer: They are easy to carry and are soft, cuddly, and cute.
2. You can look in an encyclopedia, on a CD-ROM, or in library books.
3. Grizzly, kodiak, polar, brown, black, spectacled, and Malayan are all different types of bears. You can learn about bears from encyclopedias, CD-ROMs, the Internet, and videos about bears.
4. Sample answer: Naming the stuffed bear after the popular President Roosevelt helped make the toy bear very popular.
5–6. Answers will vary.

PAGE 6

1. You have two eardrums.
2. You should have an earache checked by a doctor.
3. Listening in school helps you learn. It is important to hear directions, new information, and any questions that are asked.
4. An eardrum is a thin layer of tissue that is stretched across the middle part of the ear. The musical instrument we call a drum also has material stretched across it. They both vibrate to create sound.
5. Sample answers: At music lessons, parades, concerts, and graduation ceremonies.
6. Answers will vary.

PAGE 7

1. Sample answer: You might feel a swaying sensation. Some people might feel dizzy or off balance.
2. Sample answers: The World Trade Center in New York City, the Stratosphere Tower in Las Vegas, and the Petronas Towers in Kuala Lumpur, Malaysia. You could look in an encyclopedia or almanac, or on the Internet to find others.
3. Answers will vary.
4. A tall building needs a sturdy, solid base to support it and prevent it from toppling over.
5. Sample answers: Most buildings have doors, windows, walls, floors, and a roof. They might be made of concrete, wood, brick, or glass.
6. Answers will vary.

PAGE 8

1–2. Answers will vary.
3. The puppeteer isn't seen; only his or her voice is heard. Anyone can make up a voice for the puppet that the person is controlling.
4. *Pinocchio* tells the story of a marionette who becomes a living boy.
5. Sample answer: Shy people might not want to be onstage where they can be seen. The puppet is the center of attention in a puppet show.
6. Answers will vary.

PAGE 9

1. An easel allows the painter to move his or her arm and brush freely. When painting on a flat surface, it's hard for a painter not to rub his or her arm on places that have already been painted.
2–4. Answers will vary.
5. Dutch people live in the Netherlands on the continent of Europe.
6. Answers will vary.

PAGE 10

1–2. Answers will vary.
3. Sample answer: That person can try very hard to make his or her mind think the touch will not feel ticklish. This might be a case of mind over matter.
4. Answers may vary. Scientists believe that it is very difficult to tickle oneself.
5–6. Answers will vary.

PAGE 11

1. Answers will vary.
2. Sample answers: Dust, pollen, animal dander, perfume, mold, chemical smells, and chalk dust can make people sneeze.
3. People cover their mouths to stop the spread of germs and to be polite.
4. Allergies are a body's reaction to certain substances. People sneeze more at certain times because they may be exposed to more of the items to which they are allergic.
5. Your lungs would slowly get filled up with a lot of dust, and the germs might cause you to get sick.
6. Answers will vary.

PAGE 12

1. Many different animals yawn. Sample answers: Dogs, wolves, wild and domestic cats, and gorillas.
2. People cover their mouths when they yawn to be polite. An ancient belief held that covering one's mouth kept one's life force safely inside the body.
3. When one person yawns, other people around that person usually also yawn. Scientists believe that the power of suggestion is very strong.
4. Physical activities such as walking, riding a bike, jumping rope, and running bring oxygen into the body.
5. Your body needs rest in order to function properly and to be able to fight off infections and sickness.
6. Rip Van Winkle was a fictional character who fell asleep in the Catskill Mountains for nearly 20 years. When he finally woke up, he had a long white beard and long white hair.

PAGE 13

1–2. Answers will vary.
3. People can stop getting freckles by avoiding exposure to the Sun as much as possible.
4. A person with dark skin has a lot of melanin. A person with light skin has less melanin.
5. The Sun can burn or tan a person's skin. Too much sunshine over a long period of time can cause skin cancer.
6. You can protect your skin from the Sun by wearing sunscreen, a hat, and other types of clothing that cover your skin.

PAGES 14–15

1. Sample answers: On windows, television screens, refrigerators, mirrors, doorknobs, and tabletops.
2. Vinegar and water or window cleaner washes fingerprints off a window.
3. Keeping your hands clean will help you keep your fingerprints to yourself.
4. The police use fingerprints to identify people because each person has a unique set of fingerprints. The police can help solve crimes or identify missing children by matching fingerprints.
5. Answers will vary. Note that most hospitals usually take a newborn child's handprints and footprints.
6. Animals do not have fingerprints like humans. They are identified by the footprints or tracks that they make.

PAGE 16

1. Answers will vary.
2. Seashells can be found along the shoreline of the beach, in the ocean water, and in certain stores or museums.
3. Sample answers: Crabs, lobsters, clams, oysters, abalone, snails, and turtles have shells.
4. Sample answers: Foods that have shells include crab, lobster, oysters, sunflower seeds, peanuts, and eggs.
5–6. Answers will vary.

PAGE 17

1. Chicago is in the state of Illinois. *Parent:* Make sure your child finds Illinois on a globe or a map.
2. Answers will vary.
3. A two-story Ferris wheel has one wheel on top of the other.
4. 1,680 more people.
5. Sample answers: Bicycles, tricycles, in-line skates, scooters, skateboards, and wagons.
6. Answers will vary.

PAGES 18–19

1. Sample answers: Queens approve new bills before they become laws.
2. You can look in history books, watch historical videos, and find information on the Internet.
3. Answers will vary.
4. *Royal* means having to do with a king, a queen, or their family. A prince is the son of a king or a queen, or the husband of a princess. A princess is the daughter of a king or a queen, or the wife of a prince.
5. The United States does not have a royal family. The president and the Congress, who are elected by the people, rule the country.
6. They both rule over a group of people (or bees) and have workers doing jobs for them.

PAGE 20

1. Answers will vary.
2. Snails live in damp places such as gardens, hedges, and other areas where there is plant life.
3. Sample answers: Fishworms, slugs, and inchworms move by contracting their muscles.
4. The snail is able to hold on to a thin blade of grass by secreting a sticky mucus.

5. You can place a long piece of string or yarn alongside the snail's trail, then measure it with a measuring tape. Or, you can place the measuring tape alongside the trail.
6. Answers will vary.

PAGE 21

1–3. Answers will vary.
4. When they rub their feelers, ants may be telling each other where to find food, identifying themselves, or warning each other of danger.
5. Ants might bite if they feel scared or threatened.
6. Answers will vary.

PAGE 22

1. Sample answers: At the zoo or wild animal park.
2. Skunks, tigers, snakes, fish, lizards, and cats can have stripes. Rest of answer will vary.
3. They live in zoos because the United States doesn't have natural open grasslands for them to live in.
4. Answers will vary. Various shades of green, brown, and gray might be the best colors to use if hiding in the jungle.
5. Sample answer: Pictures of each zebra's stripes could be taken and kept on file to identify them.
6. A leopard's spots help the leopard blend in with the grassy brush and trees where it lives. An alligator's body shape looks like a floating log in the rivers and swamps where it lives.

PAGE 23

1. Answers will vary.
2. Like a giraffe, an ostrich has a very long neck.
3. The spots camouflage the giraffe, helping it blend in with the trees and tall grasses around it.
4. Answers will vary.
5. When a giraffe runs, this warns other animals that danger might be near.
6. Answers will vary.

PAGE 24

1. Sample answers: Birds, coyotes, bees, crickets, and rattlesnakes can make sounds that may be used in music.
2. Sample answers: Drum, horn, piano, flute, guitar, tuba, violin, trombone, triangle, and tambourine.
3. A whistle is called a wind instrument because air is blown through it to make music.

4. Answers will vary.
5. Sample answers: Guitar, mandolin, viola, double bass or string bass, cello, and harp.
6. Answers will vary.

PAGE 25

1. Sample answer: Dogs make good pets because they are smart, friendly, playful, and good company, and they can protect people.
2. Sample answers: Roll over, sit up, shake, fetch a newspaper or slippers, and guide blind people.
3. Sample answers: Beagle, collie, greyhound, Irish terrier, bulldog, and poodle.
4–5. Answers will vary.
6. This expression means that a dog is loyal to its owner.

PAGE 26

1. Nocturnal animals are active at night and sleep during the day.
2. Predators cannot see an octopus or a skunk after they squirt or spray their protective liquids. The octopus escapes when it squirts its dark inklike liquid. A skunk's spray briefly blinds its enemy so that the skunk can escape.
3. A skunk's black-and-white coloring helps it blend in with shadows created by objects at night.
4. "That smells like a skunk" means the odor is offensive and smells bad, like a skunk's spray.
5. Stay away from the skunk. Call the local animal control center to report a skunk seen in the daytime.
6. Most common answers will use a skunk's smell as some type of warning. Some answers will be quite creative and humorous.

PAGE 27

1. Sample answers: Turtles, crocodiles, alligators, snakes, chameleons, and iguanas are reptiles.
2. Lizards live in hot, sunny climates such as the desert.
3. The lizard's home must be kept warm. In climates where temperatures are cold in winter, some type of heat source, such as a lightbulb, will be needed to keep the lizard warm.
4. Lizards eat small bugs, flies, and spiders. Encyclopedias or books about lizards will help you learn more about them.

5. A lizard's skin coloring helps camouflage it. Lizards blend in with the grass, soil, or tree bark around them.
6. Answers will vary.

PAGE 28

1. Answers will vary.
2. On a hot summer's day, long hair usually makes you feel sweaty, sticky, and hot, while short hair usually makes you feel cooler. Rest of answer will vary.
3. Sample answer: Protein foods such as milk, eggs, cheese, meats, beans, nuts, and soy products help to keep hair and nails healthy.
4. Sample answer: Long hair and nails can sometimes make a witch look scarier.
5. Long hair helps keep in body heat during cold weather. Body heat is easily lost through the top of the head.
6. Answers will vary.

PAGE 29

1. Answers will vary.
2. Bangs are easier to cut and style than many other hairstyles.
3. No, it doesn't hurt the horse because there aren't any nerves in the horse's hair.
4. Caring for a horse involves feeding, washing, drying, grooming, and exercising it, as well as cleaning out the stable where the horse lives.
5. Answers will vary.
6. Sample answer: People got the ponytail idea from horses who had their tails tied at the top.

PAGES 30–31

1–3. Answers will vary.
4. People with curly hair can never permanently straighten their hair. They can straighten it for a short while by using products from a beauty salon or by using very large curlers.
5. Sample answer: Sheep and some dogs and cats have curly or wavy hair.
6. Hair color is determined by a pigment called melanin. Encyclopedias can teach you more about hair color, and beauty magazines contain information about hair-coloring techniques.

PAGE 32

1. Sample answers: Leaves, fruit, plants, grass, and peanuts.
2. Answers will vary.

3. Africa is located east of North and South America between the Atlantic and Indian Oceans. *Parent:* Make sure your child locates Africa on a map or a globe.
4. Giraffes, zebras, buffalo, antelope, and cattle live in herds.
5. An elephant can use its trunk like a club to hit an animal.
6. Answers will vary.

PAGE 33

1. Sample answers: Mold grows on rotting food, certain cheeses, damp basement walls or floors, very old books, damp clothes left for a long time, and decaying plants.
2. Mold is usually any combination of white, green, brown, and black. The colors are caused by the types of spores.
3. No, mold does not need sunlight to grow.
4. Mold grows best in places that are damp and dark.
5. The moisture and darkness create perfect conditions for mold to grow.
6. Sample answer: Wrap a slice of moist bread or a piece of cheese in plastic wrap, then place it inside a dark cupboard.

PAGE 34

1. Sample answers: We use electricity to operate radios, alarm clocks, televisions, computers, kitchen appliances, stoves, ovens, lights, vacuum cleaners, and washers and dryers.
2. Answers will vary.
3. A spark of static electricity can jump off your body and onto another person. Both people feel a shock.
4. Answers will vary.
5. People may have used candles, lanterns, fires, and coal-burning stoves before there was electricity.
6. Answers will vary.

PAGE 35

1. People boil water to use in cooking, to make coffee or tea, and to sterilize something, which means to kill the germs.
2. Boiling water can burn you. NEVER go near boiling water without adult supervision. Be sure an adult turns the handle of the pot inward so that it's not hanging over the edge of the stove.

3. Water molecules move slower and slower as ice is formed.
4. Ice cubes melt and turn back into a liquid when they are heated. If you continue to heat liquid, it will boil and turn into a vapor, called *steam*.
5. The molecules in ice cream move more slowly as they freeze. Rest of answer will vary.
6. Answers will vary.

PAGE 36

1. Italy is on the continent of Europe.
2. Sample answers: At parties, sports events, picnics, birthdays, and for dessert.
3. Answers will vary.
4. Freezers prevent ice cream from melting and let people store it for long periods.
5. Birthday parties as we know them came from a German custom. The tradition of eating cupcakes and ice cream, as well as using one candle for each year of life, plus one more for the year to come, began on the North American continent about 200 years ago.
6. Answers will vary.

PAGE 37

1. Sample answers: Sponges are used to wash dishes, clean up spills, clean bathrooms, wash cars, and more.
2. Most mops are made from sponges or spongy, yarnlike material. These materials make it easy to clean floors because they absorb water easily.
3. Sponges get dirty over time, and their dampness can provide a place for germs to grow.
4. Sponges are found in the ocean, attached to rocks, coral, or shells. These sponges are living creatures. You can learn about sponges on CD-ROMs, or in encyclopedias or nature books.
5. One sponge has more absorbing material or airholes than one paper towel.
6. Answers will vary.

PAGE 38

1. Sample answers: Merry-go-rounds, swings, and seesaws can make you feel dizzy.
2. Sample answers: Riding on a curvy road, getting up from a lying-down position too quickly, and not eating can make you feel dizzy.

3. This expression might mean that someone thinks you are silly or that you don't know what you are talking about.
4. Sample answers: Ballet dancers, acrobats, gymnasts, and ice skaters spin when they perform.
5. Sample answers: Tops, wheels, dreidels, and bottles spin.
6. Focusing your eyes directly on your hands helps to center your balance. You will not feel as dizzy, and you'll recover from the spin more quickly than when you don't focus on your hands.

PAGE 39
1. Sample answers: People usually eat french fries with hamburgers, ketchup, and a drink, or with other types of sandwiches.
2. Potatoes are also served baked, mashed, or scalloped, or as hash browns, home fries, and potato pancakes.
3. The parts of a carrot and potato that we eat grow under the ground.
4. A potato's eyes are the holes on its skin. They are undeveloped buds. A potato cannot see with its eyes.
5. Answers will vary. Each eye of a potato can start a new plant.
6. Immigrants brought them to America. Also, people who traveled into other countries brought customs and foods back to America with them.

PAGE 40
1. Sample answers: Cereal, toast, eggs, pancakes, waffles, sausage, bacon, oatmeal, and fruit are some common breakfast foods.
2. Answers will vary.
3. You should pack breakfast foods that don't need refrigeration, such as dried fruit, dry cereal, nuts, and water.
4. Babies without teeth need soft foods like mashed banana, milk, oatmeal, and creamed rice cereal.
5. Breakfast is the first meal of the day. It gives us energy to help us get through the day.
6. Answers will vary.

PAGE 41
1. No, people cannot live on the Moon because there isn't any water, air, or gravity.
2. The shapes children would describe are crescent, half, or full Moon.

3. The phases of the Moon are crescent, quarter, gibbous, and full. You can find out more by looking through a science book, on a CD-ROM, or at a science video.
4. Sample answers: Children might want to learn about craters, the first men to land on the Moon, lunar modules, lunar eclipses, the Moon's gravity, or how the Moon revolves around the Earth.
5. The Moon provides light, making it easier for us to see at night.
6. Answers will vary.

PAGES 42–43
1. The last stage in the picture. A total eclipse shows only the *corona,* the bright circle around the Sun, shining from behind the Moon.
2. Answers will vary.
3. The darkness of a solar eclipse fools animals into thinking that it is nighttime.
4. Your thumb can block out a larger object, just as the Moon is able to block out a larger object—the Sun.
5. Because the Moon is much closer to the Earth than the Sun is, it is able to block out the entire Sun from our view during an eclipse.
6. Sunglasses protect our eyes from the burning rays of the Sun. You can learn more in science books or encyclopedias.

PAGE 44
1. Sample answers: Any electric-powered device, battery-operated radios, calculators, watches, toys, and hand-held games need energy to work.
2. People use solar power because it is a renewable energy source that is better for our environment and natural resources.
3. A windmill uses wind, a waterwheel uses water, and a hot-air balloon uses heat as a power source.
4. Answers will vary.
5. Sample answers: Near or in a window, outside, or under an artificial light.
6. Capturing solar energy is easiest on clear summer days when the Sun is at its hottest and there are few or no clouds in the sky.

PAGE 45
1. Sample answers: The post office, schools, libraries, police stations, Olympic events, government buildings, and parades.

2. Red, white, and blue colors are on the American flag. It is designed with stars and stripes.
3. Answers will vary. Encyclopedias or books on flags contain further information.
4. *Parent:* Make sure child locates the correct symbols for these flags.
5. Sample answer: Flags bring a sense of unity and pride to the people in the group.
6. Answers will vary.

PAGES 46–47
1. Sample answers: Television, telegraph, telegram, telescope, telecommunications, telethon, telephoto, and televise.
2. Other forms of communication include letters, cards, brochures, telegraphs, radios, televisions, newspapers, magazines, walkie-talkies, pagers, E-mail, and fax machines.
3. Answers will vary. *Parent:* Make sure child knows his or her phone number. You need to know your own phone number to call home and in case of any emergency.
4. Sample answers: Cordless phones, cellular phones, car phones, old-fashioned crank telephones, videophones, and dial or touch-tone phones are all different types of telephones.
5. Sample answer: The original message in the game "Telephone" is heard and repeated by so many people that pieces of the first message are left out or changed by accident as the message is passed from person to person.
6. Dial 911 and don't hang up! The operator will ask you questions and give you important information.

PAGE 48
1–3. Answers will vary.
4. They use makeup and have learned how to use facial expressions and body movements to show different feelings.
5. Sample answers: Children may have worn makeup during Halloween, while performing in a play or a dance, or at a face-painting party.
6. Answers will vary.

PAGE 49
1. Your knee is like your elbow. It's the joint between your calf and your thigh, just like your elbow is the joint between your forearm and your biceps.

2. Answers will vary.
3. **Parent:** Make sure child points to each part of his or her own body.
4. Answers will vary.
5. Sample answers: Chicken, steak, barbecued ribs, pork chops, lamb chops, fish, duck, pheasant, turkey, and ham are all foods that can have bones attached.
6. Answers will vary.

PAGE 50
1–2. Answers will vary.
3. Teething is when teeth push their way up through the gums. Yes, puppies teethe. You can tell this by the fact that they constantly chew on everything around them.
4. Brushing after every meal and after sweet, sticky snacks, flossing, and eating healthy foods are ways to care for your teeth.
5. Some people believe that the tooth fairy takes a child's tooth from under his or her pillow at night and replaces it with a small gift. Rest of answer will vary.
6. Answers will vary.

PAGE 51
1. Answers will vary.
2. A shark uses its gills to breathe underwater.
3. People need air to breathe and could drown if they fell asleep in water.
4. Answers will vary.
5. You swim mostly at the surface of the water, swimming underwater only as long as you're able to hold your breath. You use your arms and legs to move yourself through the water. A fish uses its tail and fins.
6. Answers will vary.

PAGE 52
1. Sample answers: Whales eat krill, plankton, and crustaceans.
2. Sample answers: Humpback whale, gray whale, killer whale, blue whale, sperm whale, and bottlenose whale. CD-ROMs, encyclopedias, and animal books have further information.
3. Answers will vary.

4. Whales are mammals and need to surface and breathe air.
5. Sample answers: Large aquariums, marine parks, and on whale-watching trips on the ocean along migration routes.
6. A whale could die if it's trapped underwater for too long, because it needs air to breathe. Rest of answer will vary.

PAGE 53
1. You can look in an encyclopedia, on a CD-ROM, or in library books. Sample answers: Annie Oakley, Calamity Jane, Wild Bill Hickok, Wyatt Earp, Buffalo Bill, and Jesse James.
2. Cowboys and cowgirls herd cows, groom and shoe horses, clean stalls, repair fences, and more.
3. Cattle are animals, such as cows, raised for food.
4. Cow magnets are fed to cows to attract metallized garbage they might have accidentally eaten. The magnet and garbage are then eliminated when the cow has a bowel movement.
5. Cows provide milk and cream. Cattle provide beef.
6. Answers will vary.

PAGE 54
1. Sample answers: Sneakers, cleats, sandals, slippers, moccasins, workboots, dress shoes, high-heeled shoes, hiking boots, cowboy boots, and ballet, jazz, and tap shoes.
2. Shoes are made of many materials because they are used for various reasons. A ballet dancer needs a very different type of shoe than a construction worker does.
3. Horseshoes protect a horse's hooves.
4. Answers will vary.
5. Sample answers: Water socks, sandals, thongs, or flip-flops.
6. Cats and dogs have spongy pads on their feet for protection.

PAGE 55
1–2. Answers will vary.
3. When the edible part of a vegetable grows underground, it is called a root vegetable. Onions grow underground.
4. Sample answers: Garlic, potatoes, cucumbers, corn, oranges, grapefruit, bananas, kiwi fruit, and melons.

5. People cry when they are sad, angry, physically or emotionally hurt, or afraid.
6. Answers will vary.

PAGE 56
1. Blind people use Seeing Eye dogs, canes, their ears and sense of touch, and other people's help to get around.
2. You can learn by using your other senses, asking questions, reading braille, and getting around with the help of a Seeing Eye dog and a cane.
3. People wear glasses to help them see more clearly.
4. Eyes need to be checked regularly so that any eye problems can be detected and corrected. Doctors examine our eyes with special instruments, equipment, and eye charts.
5. Sample answers: Pin-the-tail-on-the-donkey, blindman's bluff, and hide-and-seek.
6. Answers will vary.

PAGE 57
1–3. Answers will vary.
4. Sample answers: Keep televisions and radios turned down, and keep your voice down.
5. Sample answers: Air pollution, water pollution, and beach pollution.
6. Answers will vary.

PAGE 58
1. Answers will vary.
2. Sample answers: In a bathtub, in a kitchen sink, at a car wash, and in a glass of soda.
3. The colors fade and eventually the bubble pops. This happens because as the bubble thins, the longest waves of light disappear, causing the colors to fade. The shorter ones then disappear, and finally the bubble bursts.
4. You will see more color in a bubble on a bright, sunny day because the sunlight helps bring out the colors in the bubble.
5. Answers will vary.
6. Soap and water, and an instrument to blow air through and create bubble shapes.

Mokena Community Public Library District

Other

books that will help develop your child's gifts and talents

Workbooks:
- Reading (4–6) $4.95
- Math (4–6) $4.95
- Language Arts (4–6) $4.95
- Puzzles & Games for Reading and Math (4–6) $3.95
- Puzzles & Games for Reading and Math, Book Two (4–6) $4.95
- Puzzles & Games for Critical and Creative Thinking (4–6) $4.95
- Reading Book Two (4–6) $4.95
- Math Book Two (4–6) $4.95
- Phonics (4–6) $4.95
- Phonics Puzzles & Games (4–6) $4.95
- Math Puzzles & Games (4–6) $4.95
- Reading Puzzles & Games (4–6) $4.95
- Math (6–8) $3.95
- Language Arts (6–8) $4.95
- Puzzles & Games for Reading and Math (6–8) $3.95
- Puzzles & Games for Critical and Creative Thinking (6–8) $3.95
- Puzzles & Games for Reading and Math, Book Two (6–8) $3.95
- Phonics (6–8) $4.95
- Phonics Puzzles & Games (6–8) $4.95
- Reading Comprehension (6–8) $4.95

Reference Workbooks:
- Word Book (4–6) $3.95
- Almanac (6–8) $3.95
- Atlas (6–8) $3.95
- Dictionary (6–8) $3.95

Story Starters:
- My First Stories (6–8) $3.95
- Stories About Me (6–8) $3.95
- Stories About Animals (6–8) $4.95

Science Workbooks:
- The Human Body (4–6) $5.95
- Animals (4–6) $5.95

Question & Answer Books:
- The Gifted & Talented® Question & Answer Book for Ages 4–6 $5.95
- The Gifted & Talented® Question & Answer Book for Ages 6–8 $5.95
- Gifted & Talented® More Questions & Answers for Ages 4–6 $5.95
- Gifted & Talented® More Questions & Answers for Ages 6–8 $5.95
- Gifted & Talented® Still More Questions & Answers for Ages 4–6 $5.95

Drawing Books:
- Learn to Draw (6 and up) $5.95

Readers:
- Double the Trouble (6–8) $7.95
- Time for Bed (6–8) $7.95

For Parents:
- How to Develop Your Child's Gifts and Talents During the Elementary Years $11.95
- How to Develop Your Child's Gifts and Talents in Math $15.00
- How to Develop Your Child's Gifts and Talents in Reading $15.00
- How to Develop Your Child's Gifts and Talents in Vocabulary $15.00
- How to Develop Your Child's Gifts and Talents in Writing $15.00